WOWED!

WOWED!

USING THE PRINCIPLES OF WOW TO FORGE THE ULTIMATE CUSTOMER EXPERIENCE

BY GARY JOHNSON, M.A. MBA

TATE PUBLISHING
AND ENTERPRISES, LLC

Wowed!

Published by Tate Publishing & Enterprises, LLC
127 E. Trade Center Terrace | Mustang, Oklahoma 73064 USA
1.888.361.9473 | www.tatepublishing.com

Tate Publishing is committed to excellence in the publishing industry. The company reflects the philosophy established by the founders, based on Psalm 68:11,
"The Lord gave the word and great was the company of those who published it."

Cover design by Britney Voorhees
Interior design by Jimmy Sevilleno

Published in the United States of America

ISBN: 978-1-62902-457-8
1. Business & Economics / Customer Relations
2. Business & Economics / General
13.11.08

DEDICATION

This book is dedicated to my wonderful wife, Sharon, who has always supported me in everything I have ever done. Behind every successful man, there is always a great woman who is encouraging, motivating, listening, helping, prodding, and, most importantly, loving. Thanks for always being there for me, dear. Without you, I would have never achieved my potential.

I also want to thank my parents, Suzanne and Gary, and my in-laws, Nancy and Albert. You all have been great role models, and I appreciate everything you have done for me. I also must mention my wonderful kids and how very proud I am of every one of them.

Lastly, I want to thank God for giving me a wonderful life and blessing me with more than I deserve.

CONTENTS

FOREWORD

The business climate has changed significantly over the last decade. Global competition and advancements in the Internet have changed the way in which customers research, purchase, and interact with the companies they do business with each and every day. The quality of the training provided to frontline workers has never been more important. While many leaders and business owners understand the value of connecting with the customer, the person serving the customer may not and, in many instances, just doesn't care. We have become a service industry with a lack of emphasis on "service" actually provided.

This book is designed to help navigate the ever-changing world of successful business management using the principles of "Wow." Wow is providing an overall experience that stands apart from any the customer is used to receiving, an experience that makes the customer feel special. The book provides a road map for success with wow in three main areas: business leadership, marketing, and, finally and most importantly, the overall customer experience.

The wow factor and how to apply it is at the very core of what this book will provide you and your team. The key is not only to expose your team to these principles but build a culture that will maintain the momentum of these ideals now and into the future. Remember, it is great service that has proven to differentiate every great business in every industry all over the world. Congratulations on your decision to wow your customers!

CHAPTER 1

IT ALL STARTS WITH YOU

I have been fortunate to read many great leadership books in my lifetime. Many of which have shaped me as a person and have made a huge impact on my life. One of the best books on leading that I have ever read was written by a former navy man. The book is titled *Its Your Ship*, and it was written by Captain Michael Abrashoff. In the book,

Captain Abrashoff describes his tour of duty as the captain of the *USS Benfold* during the Persian Gulf crisis. The *Benfold* is a destroyer in the United States naval fleet and, by all accounts, one of the most sophisticated ships in the navy. A destroyer is nearly the length of two football fields and has more firepower than ten ships combined from only twenty years earlier. The *Benfold*, as with any other destroyer, is manned with approximately three hundred sailors. In 1992, when Captain Abrashoff was first boarding the ship, he watched the other captain exit the *Benfold* with a series of cheers from the crew, which were more like boos (they were excited to get rid of him). *What a way to start your first day on the job.* Coming to work on your first day in which the crew that will work for you is effectively booing the person you are superseding. According to Abrashoff, the crew of a naval ship is made up of all types of sailors. One group has joined the navy because they are running from something. They are running from a bad family life, bad neighborhoods, or an overall bad circumstance. Another group of sailors on a ship are there because someone has told them they will never amount to anything, so they better join the service. The last group that makes up the crew are the sailors that joined the navy because they are patriots and simply want to serve their country. This, as you can imagine, is a very interesting group to lead collectively. This group would not be nearly as difficult to manage in a private organization because one could simply "clean house" and put in place more of the people that a leader wanted to lead. This however is not quite so simple in the navy. A captain can't just fire members of the crew because they don't fit his or her concept of the ideal sailor. There is a very detailed protocol that must be followed to remove or promote a sailor. Therefore, Abrashoff would have to lead the majority of this group during his tenor.

When Captain Abrashoff came aboard, he was taking control of a mediocre ship—mediocre in terms of its combat readiness, which is the main way in which all naval ships are measured. His sailors were not reenlisting at high rates. In fact, when he came aboard, only 30 percent of the sailors that could reenlist did so at a cost of approximately $100,000 to US taxpayers for recruiting and training each sailor's replacement. If you do the math on this, it is an incredible cost in training almost $21 million every four to six years. Before the end of Captain Abrashoff's first year, the ship went from middle of the pacific fleet in combat readiness to number 1! Not only that, but the total number of sailors on the ship that were reenlisting went from only 30 percent to 100 percent. Let me repeat that, 100 percent! This was the same group of sailors that were booing the previous captain off the ship. When I explain this to people in my lectures, I always remind them not to discount Captain Abrashoff's results as simply a matter of being a brilliant or charismatic leader. In fact, Abrashoff said he was lucky to graduate from the naval academy. Based on his success, I would still argue he is brilliant, but his brilliance was in building a winning team, something anyone with some solid training and commitment can achieve.

So what is my point? I have bad news and good news as you read this book. The bad news is that if your business or business unit is not as successful as you would like it to be, the person staring back at you in the mirror each morning is ultimately responsible. Now unusual market conditions can surely occur, but that does not mean you have to become a victim of your circumstance. Many businesses have found ways to grow even in the most challenging economies (just look at the history of companies that were founded during the great declines: Disney, GE, and Microsoft to name just a few), which leads me to the good news of this book. Captain Abrashoff proved that if you are not happy with your current circumstance, you can change it in very short order if you are committed to making a change.

I ask many of my clients through out the year, "What do think is the biggest challenge you have in business today?" I get many answers, but most fall into just a few categories. One of the most common challenges I hear about relates to staff—specifically, the management and leadership of those integral members of the team. It includes keeping the team on the same page, managing conflict, and ensuring that every one member of the team is focused on the same set of standards.

As the captain of your ship, it is critical that you and your leadership team bring a great attitude to work every day. In fact, it is your own attitude as a leader that ultimately dictates the attitude of your team. We have been told for thousands of years in almost every culture that we as humans are what we think about. Norman Vincent Peale, author of *The Power of Positive Thinking*, said it best over fifty years ago when he said that our minds are like fertile farm ground. We can plant something positive or poisonous; then, the mind will grow either one without prejudice. Zig Ziglar, arguably the most recognizable name in personal growth management, said, "Your attitude not your aptitude will determine your altitude!" So getting your own attitude right will impact your growth, employee morale, and even the business decisions you will make that will impact your business for years to come. This most likely does not come as news to you but being reminded how critical your leadership attitude is and how much impact it has own the success of your business cannot be denied.

Now that we have established the impact of your own attitude on the success of your business, what about the attitude of your team members? I think you would agree it is as critical to the success of your business as your own attitude. Knowing this is true, how can you ensure your employees are serving your customer with the proper mindset? Well, this entire book is ultimately dedicated to that one objective, but let's tackle one of the issues we must manage in our business—stress. Stress can be behind many of the negative emotions or attitudes that creep into your business. The key is to recognize those things that contribute to stress within your business walls and minimize them on a daily basis. As a business leader in charge of other human beings, I am sure you would agree that at some point, your employee or employees will encounter things in their personal life that can impact their work life. These things may include relationship issues, money issues, family crisis, dog issues, car problems, you name it, and at some point, you will probably encounter it as you lead people. Here is the key to personal life stress—you can't do anything about it. It is not your role to lecture your employees about the decisions they make at home. They are individuals and will find that no matter what we tell them, life will throw them a curve ball. The key however is to ensure that we do not let that personal life stress find its way into our business. Of course, we should be compassionate and caring, but we must ensure we build a culture that says, "Come to work, and go on vacation from your problems." Additionally, we need to make sure that the culture we have established in our businesses minimize the undue stress that can be caused by things we can control or reduce in our business. According to a study conducted by the Economic Roundtable on Mental Health,[1] there are ten factors that have been rank ordered based on the impact they have on causing employee stress.

Number 10 on the list is *too much or too little to do*. We can all probably agree that having too much to do can be extremely stressful, but what about too little to do? If you think about it, not being busy enough can actually be more detrimental to your business. Humans learn best through repetition, and not having someone utilizing the power of repetition can cause unforced errors or a poor workmanship. For example, let's assume that someone in your family has been told that they have a clogged artery in their heart. Would they seek out an expert cardiologist that does two to three weekly surgeries like the one your family member requires, or would they

1 Monica Nolan, June 2009, http://www.peoplemetrics.com/blog/top-ten-sources-of-workplace-stress-and-how-to-fight-them.

give the family practitioner a crack at it? Repetition builds expertise. Having knowledge without regularly performing tasks is not very valuable unless you are in a classroom teaching.

Number 9 on the list is *too many interruptions.* All of us like to complete tasks. It gives us a feeling of accomplishment. Unfinished tasks can cause anxiety. So people like to take on projects that can be accomplished quickly. This is why we usually knock off the easy stuff on our to-do lists on the weekend. Keep in mind as the leader of your business that big, long and cumbersome projects can feel overwhelming to your team. Be sure to break these projects down into very manageable sections that can then be checked off the list. This will make even the most challenging project feel much more manageable for your team.

Number 8 on the list of stressors in the workplace is *uncertainty.* Many organizations do not let their teams know how the business is doing or what impact they as an individual or as a department are having on the overall success (or failure) of the business. Be sure as a leader to let the team know how the business is doing and share key data on growth, goal accomplishment, and individual performance.

Number 7 on the list is *vicious office politics.* Chemistry is one of the most critical elements of success on any team. Having members of the team that are rude, not team players, or simply not able to connect with the rest of your staff should never be tolerated. These cons outweigh any potential pro their individual skills may bring. Just study the profile of Terrell Owens, one of the NFL's greatest wide receivers, to understand the impact of team chemistry. Although he had great individual skills, his inability to get along with his teammates has tarnished his reputation and caused him to struggle to find a permanent team.

Number 6 on the list of employment stress is *unclear expectations.* Research is very clear on this issue. Not setting clear expectations is not only a top stressor, but it is one of the main reasons that organizations fail to consistently achieve their objectives.

It is critical to set the standard of service you and your organization demand and then hold your entire team to that standard.

The number 5 stressor in the work place is *job and career ambiguity*. Not much to say on this one as it relates fairly close to the point made regarding setting clear expectations. Be sure to frequently sit down with each of your key team members and talk with them about their career goals and how your organization can help move them toward those goals or even fulfill them. Be sure your employees clearly understand the impact they as individuals are having on the organization.

No feedback, good or bad, comes in as the number 4 stressor. Feedback is critical for humans to achieve high-level results in areas of life but especially in business. Let me give you an example. I have four children; my youngest once played in a basketball league that did not keep score. I am not sure if you have experienced one of these events, but more focus is put on acclimating the players to the sport over winning or losing. At the end of the game, I went up to my son and said, "You guys played great!"

My son looked at me and said, "Dad, we won by six baskets!" Here is the management principle that can be learned from this everyday life event. At ten years old, we try to take away the scoreboard, and what do humans do? They keep score. Creating business scoreboards is critical if you want to get the members of your team to become self-managed. Determine three to five key things you would like to measure and start publicly tracking it and talking about it. In very short order, your team will begin watching those scoreboards and will use them to shape their behavior and activities.

Coming in number 3 on the list of stressors is *no appreciation*. We will really focus on this point throughout the book but in short, your team really wants to feel like you as the leader appreciate them on a personal and business level. Your employees cannot read your mind and really value hearing from you how much they are appreciated. Be sure to specifically tie that feeling directly to a behavior; that way, the employee can understand clearly what they did to receive your praise so that they can repeat it.

The number 2 stressor in the work place is a *lack of communication*. Our employees are telling us here that we are not very good listeners. We may listen well to our customers but not very well to them. This can be true especially as it relates to their ideas that could improve the service or quality of our business. Be sure to be known more for asking your employees questions than making statements—questions like, "How would you handle this?" or "What should we do to improve this?"

The number 1 stressor in the workplace is *no sense of control*. Think of how stressful it would be to not have the ability as a leader to have input on the direction of your company. So if it stressful for you, why would it not be stressful for your team? As Captain Abrashoff said in his book *It's Your Ship*, getting your team to see the business as their own is the best way to build long-term sustainable success. To do this, we must get our team involved in decisions we are making that impact their ability to serve or perform their job.

The last point I want to make in this chapter relates to personal development. When I say personal development, I am writing about your personal development as the leader. So many business leaders I have met with over the last ten years have spent thousands of hours in school (either formal school or the school of hard knocks) preparing for their future success yet stop learning once they reach a certain level of success. I encourage every one of my clients to stay in the learning mode. There are many ways to accomplish this goal. You can, for example, stay in the learning mode by reading books on leadership, business management, and human dynamics. You can stay in the learning mode by joining an online resource that sends you tidbits of information each day or each month that keep you current or keep you inspired. You can join a group of other business leaders that meets periodically to discuss best practices or discusses challenges. I cannot overemphasize the benefit of staying in the learning mode. It keeps you current. It forces you to think about your current business practices and how they match up to other successful companies. I often tell my clients that the enemy to becoming excellent is being really good. Really good can cause you or your organization to become complacent. Our goal as leaders should be to constantly strive to make our companies the best they can be. To make our companies the best, we as leaders must be willing to show our employees that we are still willing to learn and get better each and every day.

CHAPTER 2

CREATING THE WOW FOUNDATION

Let's assume that I am taking you on a fishing trip next weekend. Let's also assume that you have never been on a fishing trip before. Because you have never been fishing, you head off to the local sporting goods store to obtain your fishing gear. You purchase a beautiful new rod and reel and a multitude of lures that are sure to catch the ultimate fish. As we head onto the water and begin fishing, you notice that I am catching fish after fish, while you struggle to get any bites. My line sits in the water and gets bites, while you constantly throw your line into the water and reel it in empty. Finally, you get the nerve as a new angler to ask me why you are not having the same success I am. I look at your equipment and say, "We are here to fish the bottom for catfish, and you are using top water lures that never leave the surface of the water." Now you may be thinking this is a silly example and you would never come to a fishing expedition without first asking what type of gear to buy. This scenario, however, happens all the time in small business. The business owner or marketing person are not exactly sure what their right client looks like, so they use a multitude of marketing ideas looking for the one that's effective. The problem with this approach is that it is expensive, time consuming, and very inefficient. What all businesses must do before they begin marketing their business is first determine who they are trying to market to or attract. This can only be done by carefully examining your past history, looking closely at patterns of client behavior that help you determine what your right clients looks like before you ever try and market your product or services. You can't consistently catch catfish unless you are fishing in the right place with the right bait. The same is true of marketing your business. Be sure you know who you are trying to attract to ensure marketing success. Hoping your marketing works without doing your due diligence is not a good strategy. Look at your customer data to determine which of your customers are your most loyal and profitable. You will most likely find patterns you can use to market to existing and future customers that fit the same criteria.

While attracting new customers is always important, business owners and leaders have long known that servicing your current customers at an exceptional level is one of the best ways to grow and market your business. Wowed customers spend more money with you and tell their friends to do business with your company. One of the best ideas I have seen on wowing existing customers and employees comes from Nido Qubein. Nido's background is an incredible story of success. A self-made man originally from the Middle East, Nido has become one of the most sought after speakers on developing the ultimate business culture. His resumé would be impressive compared to anyone. He has written more than a dozen books, serves as president of High Point University, is the chairman of Great Harvest Bread Company, and sits on several high profile boards of directors. He is also a member of the International Speakers Hall of Fame.

When Nido was asked to come back to his alma mater as president, one of the first things he wanted to do was ensure the experience his students and faculty were receiving on a regular basis was incredible. That is why he designated one of his employees as director of wow. In addition to their regular duties, the director of wow was assigned the responsibility of finding ways to delight the students and the faculty. One of the first ideas the newly appointed director recommended related to the student experience. After surveying the campus, the employee noticed that there were dirt pathways all around the campus that the students were using to reduce the time necessary to get around the school. When this was mentioned to Nido, the employee said the she felt the students were telling them where the pathways should be. Nido agreed and gave her full authority to put in beautiful pathways to replace the dirt ones. There is valet parking for the students after 9:00 p.m. for enhanced security. There are free car washes for students on the weekend and an ice cream truck that meanders the campus. University freshman enrollment has tripled and so has the school's endowment.[2] The focus on wowing the student or

2 Todd Cohen, "High Point University Focuses on Wow," April 2007. http://www.philanthropyjournal.org/archive/130157.

in reality the university's customer is paying huge dividends for High Point. It can do the same for your business. Appoint someone on your team to be your business unit's or company's director of wow. Have them read the story online about the success High Point has had with this approach for inspiration and, lastly, support them in their endeavors to wow your customers. Give them the authority to implement the ideas they come up with and watch the magic happen.

GETTING YOUR TEAM'S INPUT FOR IMPORTANT DECISIONS

For many years, successful leaders have been able to leave one business and join another and repeat their success. Many people suggest this is because they have great ideas. But is it really the idea that makes them a great leader or is it their ability to get their team to "implement" or buy into the idea? I suggest it's the latter and not the former. Research was done several years ago that showed that millions of dollars were spent in the late 1990s and early 2000s by companies who hired consultants to come in and make recommendations for improvement to their business. When follow-up studies were done to evaluate the impact of these ideas, very few were shown to be significantly successful. Is this because the ideas these highly qualified consultants came up with were bad? No, in fact many of the ideas were outstanding. The problem came down to the execution stage. While the ideas were good, the buy-in by those who had to carry out the ideas on a daily basis was not established well in those companies who saw little to no results from the recommended changes.

In over fifteen years of facilitating lectures, corporate strategic planning sessions, and board of directors meetings, the best way I have seen to gain group input and buy-in is done the following way. First, determine what issue you or your organization wants to tackle. It could be literally any subject. It could be how to reduce expenses, increase sales, improve service, or any other important business decision. Once you have established the issue you would like to address, call a staff meeting. Once you have brought your team together, position a flip chart at the front of the room with the topic you want to cover written at the top of the page. Explain to the group that the organization has a challenge that needs to be addressed, and you want to get their feedback on how to handle the challenge. Break your staff into groups of three to five employees. Establish a team leader for the exercise for each team.

Use something quantifiable to identify each team's leader. It could be the person with the oldest car, most pets, or longest commute; it really does not matter. Once each team has established their team leader, explain to the group that they will be brainstorming how to tackle the challenge you have put on the flip chart. Each group's team leader will be their team's spokesperson and scribe for the exercise. Remind the group that no one is to judge the ideas that come up on each team; simply document each idea in the allotted time. It is important to stay away from the word "how" when brainstorming and replace with the phrase "In what ways." This may sound subtle, but the word "how" implies that the idea must work. This inhibits brainstorming, and avoiding it when describing the exercise is very important.

Here is an example of how this would sound, "As a team determine *in what ways* we can increase sales for our division over the next ninety days." After the team has been given their instruction, ask them to start brainstorming. This process is incredible. It literally has worked every time I have used it in well over five hundred workshops. As the teams sit together and brainstorm ideas, your role as the meeting facilitator is to give the group about seven to ten minutes to come up with their suggestions. After this period, ask the teams to stop. Ask the team leaders to tally the number of ideas they have. Quickly go around the room and find out how many ideas each team has generated. After you have done this, explain to the group that you want them to know, go back to their list of ideas, and pick their favorite two ideas from their list. Explain they will only be given five minutes to do this.

The reason the groups have been limited on deliberation time is intentional. If you give a group a short amount of time to pick, they will usually come to consensus on two ideas very quickly. The ideas they pick are almost always the two ideas that everyone agrees stand apart from the rest. After each group picks their favorite two ideas, ask them to again stop. As you stand at the flip chart, write each group's favorite two ideas on the paper. Consolidate any duplicate ideas. At this point, you should have anywhere from two to twelve ideas on the flip chart depending on the size of your group. Now that you have all of these ideas on the chart, explain to the group that you would like to leave the meeting with the goal of implementing one idea from those listed on the paper. To do so, you would like to ask everyone in the room to individually vote for their favorite two ideas. Let them know that you will be voting by a show of hands, and therefore, you want to read the list of ideas to the group, ask them to consider their favorite two ideas, and then you will come back to the group and get their votes.

After you have read the list to the group, call out each idea by itself and then ask for a show of hands from the people in the group that have chosen that idea as their favorite. Write down the number of votes next to each idea. By the end of this exercise, one idea will stand out as best. If two ideas tie for best, revote on the two ideas asking the group to pick only one. If they are still tied, implement both ideas. Again, I have performed this brainstorming session well over five hundred times, and each and every time, it has produced an idea or two that the group agrees on. This is key because it is the team's idea, not yours. Research shows us the team will be much more successful implementing an idea when they own it. Look at it this way—ideas are like small children; everyone loves their own.

HOLD YOUR TEAM TO A HIGHER STANDARD

Sports have really been overused to make points about business strategy, but it is hard to resist the temptation because there are many parallels between the two. Vince Lombardi was just recently recognized by ESPN as the greatest football coach ever. What an honor. There have been so many great football coaches in the history of the game and to be the named the best ever surely makes him smile down at us from the great football field in the sky. It also fits perfectly with his mindset as a coach. Vince was known for many sayings that represent how he felt about winning and losing. One of the more famous sayings was, "There is no room for second place. There is only one place in my game, and that is first place." He was known for setting the highest expectations for his teams, and history shows that it paid off. Vince Lombardi was one of the most successful coaches of all time in the regular season but more importantly in the playoffs. In ten playoff games, he was 9–1. So what can we learn from this sports legend? We can learn that our teams can never reach their potential unless we first demand it of them. I don't mean we have to scream and yell at them and make them run sprints if they fail to meet our expectations, but we certainly must first ask them to reach for more, more than they would if they were simply self-directed. History proved it. In almost every case, humans perform better when coached and challenged to be their best. If your business is going to achieve its greatest potential, we must first set that as the goal. Anything less and you will normally get less.

As I mentioned earlier in the book, humans will want to know how they are doing and will go to great lengths to find out. This principle can truly help you as a business leader. Remember that the more scoreboards you create for your team that measures their impact, the more they will self-manage to those scoreboards.

When I was in business school, our professors drilled it into our heads that the only way to manage something was first be able to measure it. If not, you were simply guessing, and guessing is not a successful long-term business strategy. Determine in your business or area of responsibility the four to five things you want to measure, and put those measurements in plain view and talk about them constantly.

PROTECT YOUR MOST IMPORTANT ASSET

I ask business owners and leaders throughout the country to tell me what they feel is their most important asset. Many answer that it is their customer, and on the surface, that would seem right. However, if the person you have serving your most important asset does a poor job, then your assets would dwindle very quickly. That is why I argue that the most important asset for any business is their employees. Without a great group of these people, you are in trouble. Think about it this way; it is great that the CEO of Disney thinks that creating a wow experience for the guest is critical, and you would expect that. However, if the people serving the guest throughout the day do not share that same passion, then the experience is indelibly tarnished.

So it is the employees on your team that are without question the most important asset to your organization. It is they that will color the overall impression of your business. That being said, the real challenge is ensuring you first have the right team members. Jim Collins talked about this same point in his book *Good to Great* when he said you must get the right people on the bus and the wrong people off the bus. His point is that successful organizations must first have the right talent. Without outstanding attitudes and talent, even the greatest plans can fail. So ask yourself, does everyone on your team scores at least a 9 on a scale of 1–10 in attitude with 10 being the highest possible score? If not, why are they working for you, and more importantly, why are they interacting with your customers or potential customers? One of the most common issues I hear when conducting seminars with business owners, relates to the challenge of managing people, especially as it relates to motivating them. Over the last thirty years, there have been quite a few studies done on this very subject. Interestingly, the top motivators in the workplace have vacillated over the years depending on economic conditions, age of the work force, etcetera. However, two of the top motivators in a recent McKinsey study[3] showed that the top motivators were praise from the boss

3 Lisa Quast, "The Best Ways to Motivate Employees (and It Isn't Money)," March 2011, http://www.forbes.com/sites/lisaquast/2011/03/07/the-best-ways-to-motivate-people-and-it-isnt-with-money/.

and attention from leadership. This is not surprising as many studies over the last thirty years have cited sincere appreciation from the boss as the number 1 motivator. Don't get me wrong; money and benefits are motivators and usually make the top ten but are never number 1. In fact, money has a tendency to be viewed more as an entitlement than a motivator (I am getting paid more because I deserve it or earned it). Praise and attention from the boss, however, are not viewed the same way. These are relational in nature and have a tendency to be much stronger and deeper in motivating long term.

To make this point, I want to share with you an excerpt from Captain Abrashoff's book *It's Your Ship* that makes my point. I do not think I can say it any better than he does:

> I began writing letters to the parents, especially when their sons or daughters did something I could honestly praise. When the letters arrived, the parents invariably called their children to say how proud they were of them.

> To this day, I get Christmas cards from grateful parents.
>
> One young man who wasn't star material was working on a project with four outstanding sailors. I debated whether he deserved one of my letters; because he was part of a stellar group, I went ahead. His parents were divorced, so I sent a letter to each parent. About two weeks later, the sailor knocked on my door with tears streaming down his face.
>
> "What's wrong?" I asked. "I just got a call from my father, who all my life told me I'm a failure. This time, he said he'd just read your letter, and he wanted to congratulate me and say how proud he was of me. It's the first time in my entire life he's actually encouraged me. Captain, I can't thank you enough."

Here is my question to you; do you think that Captain Abrashoff had this sailor's loyalty? There is no question he had his loyalty. What did it take to earn it? A handwritten note that probably took fifteen minutes to write.

Many of the people reading this book have father wounds, and I am truly sorry for that. Many of the people working for you may also have father wounds, and I am sure you feel for them, but you can do very little to change that. What you can do is ensure they don't end up with boss wounds. These can easily be avoided by reminding your team how much you care about them. By taking the time to get to know them as an individual and what they value in life and by challenging them and coaching them, they will begin to care how much you know because they know how much you care.

The greatest asset we all have as business leaders and owners are the people who represent us every day.

CHAPTER 3

THE FIRST ENCOUNTER

Now that we have established some basic foundational principles of developing a wow customer service experience, I want to dig even deeper. To do so, I want you to consider two critical questions when analyzing the market presence and perception of your division, business unit, or company. Question number 1: If you were to ask your staff how much money is spent each year to market your business, how do you think they would answer? Question number 2: If a potential customer were considering making a change in their current supplier or service provider, how many possible interactions could she have with your business during her search and first encounter with your business?

Let's first address the question about annual marketing budget. If you asked your staff how much is spent each year to market the business unit or division of your business, what would they say? Do you think they would say $50,000? How about $100,000? Well, in either case, they would not even be close. Here is why. Let's say you just came back from a marketing seminar at the local university. In that seminar, the marketing expert told the audience that if they plan on being in business over the next fifteen years and don't have a strong web presence, they are in big trouble.

The reason for this is because research shows us that 89 percent of people will search the Internet before making a purchasing decision.[4] In addition to being on the web, the expert goes on to say that not only must you have a presence, but you must be within the first two pages of their search or they won't find you. This is because recent research from Google shows that 60 percent of all clicks on a search come in the first six spots on page 1. This means that search engine (SEO) and RSS (Really Simply Syndication) are an absolute must in the development of your site.

The marketing expert goes on to describe the critical nature of choosing your meta-description tag wisely. A meta-description tag is the sentence or two underneath your business name on an Internet search. Most businesses unfortunately allow the search engine to randomly pull information from your site to place in your metadata. The marketing expert strongly recommends that you prepare these

4 Brafton Editorial, "89 Percent of Consumers Use Search Engines for Purchase Decisions," February 2012, http://www.brafton.com/news/89-percent-of-consumers-use-search-engines-for-purchase-decisions.

words wisely as this is what the searcher is reading to determine which site to click on.

In addition to search engine optimization, really simple syndication, and the metadata, the marketing guru tells the audience that research shows that once someone clicks on your site, you have less than seven seconds to make an impression before the searcher will hit the "back" button.[5] This means that things like coloring and ability to easily navigate your site are critical. Other important considerations include: pictures of staff, clearly demonstrating what makes your business unique, and answering frequently asked questions.

Now, armed with this new information, you go back to your business and make changes to your web-site as suggested by the marketing consultant. You hire your region's most expert website developer. You bring someone in from the novel writing department at the local university to write the metadata and to

5 Joe Kalinowski, "Seven Seconds to Make an Impression," September 2011, http://socialtract.com/2011/09/seven-seconds-to-make-an-impression-website-design-tips/.

reconstruct all wording throughout the site. You hire an interior decorator to make recommendations on the right colors for each web page. You send the staff to the mall to get their pictures taken by Glamour Shots. The site now truly looks incredible.

Now that your site is ready and available to view by the world, let's go back and answer the question about your annual marketing budget. Your potential customer is in search of a new vendor or service provider. She goes to the Internet and finds your site on page one of her search. The meta tag underneath your business name catches her attention. She reads it and cannot wait to click on your site. She clicks and truly cannot believe the beautiful coloring of your site. The words on the site are like poetry. Every question she has is answered with flair and precision. She notices pictures of your staff and imagines how wonderful they will be to deal with. Everything about your site tells her she has found the ideal company. She hurriedly dials the phone with great anticipation of the beginning of a long and wonderful relationship. Then everything comes to a screeching halt when the person on your end of the line answers and sounds like Bonnie Bad Day or Nancy Negative. What happened to all the money you spent to attract this potential new patient to your site? It went right down the drain.

We as humans are emotional decision makers and every encounter with us is measured and analyzed.[6] A potential customer will make decisions on whom they will pick to do business with based on how your team makes them feel. Let me give you an example of how this works. The illustration 1.1 represents an emotional continuum for a human being.

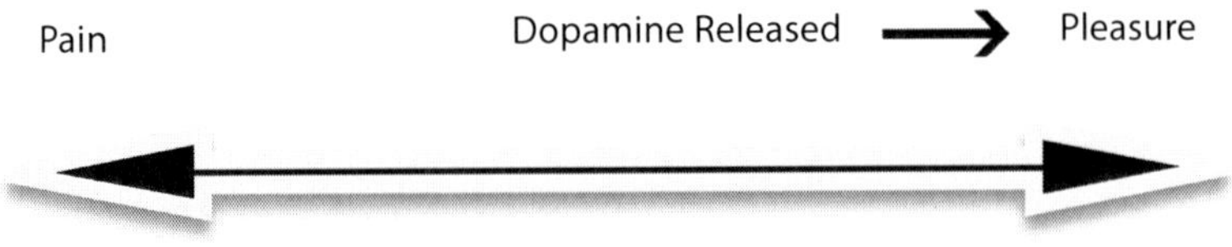

Illustration 1.1

6 Gallup Business Journal, "The Business Impact of Human Emotions," November 2012, http://businessjournal.gallup.com/content/158450/business-impact-human-emotions.aspx.

Humans will always make decisions that move them closer to the pleasure end of the continuum or away from the pain end. We do this subconsciously. No matter how logical we think we are as decision makers. Here is why. Each of us as humans have different life experiences that impact what we see as pleasurable and what we see as painful. Let us say for an example that someone you know has always been in relationships that end up going poorly. The brain then associates getting close to someone as potentially painful. Then as a defense mechanism, that person you know begins to do things to sabotage the relationship when it looks as though a relationship is becoming too serious.

The same is true of pleasure. The brain likes the feeling of the pleasure and will do things even subconsciously to move closer to the pleasure side of the continuum. Now thinking about your business, your potential customer, is also emotional in her decision-making. Making good decisions for her business, her team or even her family are almost always on the pleasure side of the continuum. So when she decides to choose your business, she will make that decision based on how your team makes her feel more than any other factor. Your customer does not always know the difference between a good service provider and a great one. In fact, being good is the price of admission in every industry. Your potential customer assumes it. So being good at what you do is simply not good enough. It does not guarantee any future business.

Therefore, it is staff that will have the greatest impact on the growth of your business. Period. No matter how good you are as a leader or business owner, no matter how much you advertise, the greatest sustainable growth factor is the perception your staff creates in the mind of the potential and current customer. That is why you should never, never, never take the first encounter for granted. Unfortunately, most businesses do not value the first encounter enough, and that is why their business success and growth are not where they would like or their customer retention numbers are below expectation.

So when considering your marketing costs, remember that your budget consists of all the money spent annually on the Internet, advertising, sponsorships, customer referral development, and, most importantly, the cost of each employee. Your team's salary is definitely part of your marketing expense because they have the greatest impact on your growth.

Now, let's consider the second question pondered earlier. You were asked to consider the number of interactions your potential customer has with your business from the time they began considering forming a relationship with your company all the way through the personal interactions they will have with your business as they make their decision to become your client. When I ask this question in seminars throughout the country, I get a wide variety of guesses from as few as one to as many as fifty. While every encounter is different, let's consider some of the more obvious interactions. When a potential customer is considering making a change in a business relationship either on a personal level or one that impacts their business, they will almost always ask their friends whom they use. This is even more prominent now with the advent of social media. This means that if your name comes positively (or negatively), it will carry significant weight as it relates to your potential customer's decision making. In fact, we all know as business leaders that the most powerful referrals we get are from wowed customers. It is their praise of our companies that can and does drive significant growth as we will discuss throughout this book.

An Internet search is also a prominent way in which a potential customer can interact with you. If you show up on page number 1 or 2 of the search, this becomes possible interaction number 2. If she reads your metadata/tag and if it intrigues her enough to click on your site, this is possible interaction number 3. If after clicking on your site, there is enough dynamic information to keep her interest, and she navigates thru it; this becomes possible interaction number 4. When I say dynamic, I am referring to video versus static information that is words. Of course, your site will require words, but be sure to add video as well. The video can be welcoming them to your site with brief explanation on how to navigate it. It could be video testimonials from other clients that chose to do business with your firm. It could be video describing and showing an important feature or benefit (or both) of your product or service. The bottom line is that brief, content-rich video is much more powerful than the same things said with just words. The key to this is keeping the video short and to the point. Many businesses are now using YouTube videos and links on their website to entertain, educate, and inform customers and potential customers of their products and services. Also, the more organic the video, the more believable it seems to be to the client. If the video resembles a commercial or infomercial, it loses credibility.

If your potential client is intrigued enough to pick up the phone and call, this becomes possible interaction number 5. If after calling, your outstanding, engaging, wow-focused front desk person who asks the right questions is pleasant and knowledgeable, this becomes possible interaction number 6. If your front desk person (or first point of contact) gets that potential customer information to the right person and immediate follow-up is conducted, this becomes possible interaction number 7. If your business sends a UPS or Federal Express ground package to the customer within three days of them making appointment to see your business or interact with your business enclosed with a handwritten note from the business owner, and a $5 Starbucks card thanking them for thinking of you, that's interaction number 8. On a sidenote, the reason I recommend a UPS or Fed Express ground package is because everyone will open a delivered package, and it always feels special when you get something delivered to your home. The gift is not as important as the handwritten note, but this idea has generated incredible goodwill from the companies I have worked with that have employed it.

When they arrive for their appointment in person and there is a sign in one of your best parking spots with their first name on it and helium balloons, this becomes possible interaction number 9. When they come in and someone from your team makes eye contact and smiles within three seconds, this becomes possible interaction number 10. If after engaging the potential customer, you offer them a drink and a quick tour of the facility, this becomes possible interaction number 11. This is the time by the way to point out anything that makes your business unique: technology, facility design, quality control, etcetera. If during the tour, the business owner stops what he or she is doing and addresses the potential customer, this becomes potential interaction number 12. What is the point? Before you have ever discussed them becoming a client, your business had at least a dozen opportunities to wow the potential customer. Are you taking those interactions for granted? I say that most businesses are missing these chances. We spend thousands of dollars to get potential customers to call us or visit us, yet we spend very little time and training for the first encounter we have spent a fortune to generate. Please remember that your customer will ultimately decide on whom she will do business with based on how your team makes her feel.

CHAPTER 4

SETTING THE SERVICE STANDARDS FOR YOUR TEAM

THE DISNEY SERVICE STANDARDS

1. Make eye contact and smile.
2. Greet and welcome each and every guest

3. Seek out guest contact.
4. Provide immediate service recovery.
5. Display appropriate body language.
6. Preserve the magical guest experience.
7. Thank each and every guest.

Whenever I conduct a seminar on the topic of this book, I always ask the audience if they have been to Disney. Invariably, there is almost always a large contingent of past Disney attendees that enthusiastically raise their hands. I then ask that group to yell out words that describe the experience. I always here words like: magical, clean, bright, amazing, friendly, Peter Pan–like, and, of course, expensive are bellowed from the crowd. Because Disney is expensive in comparison to other ways one could entertain their family, I always agree with the audience that "expensive" is definitely a word that is fair to use to describe the experience as long as you remember one thing: people are willing to spend thousands of dollars for a fun, clean, friendly, magical, Peter Pan–like experience. Not only are they willing to spend the money, they are willing to come back and spend it again (and tell all their friends how wonderful the experience was).

Since Disney does such a great job wowing their guests, I could think of no better example to follow in this book than this wonderful company. To do this, we will be going through the service standards Disney demands of their associates or cast members. Let me repeat that. They demand these standards. They are not simply said in passing or brought up once over an employee orientation; they are discussed and followed up on routinely. Below, I have outlined each service standard that we will go through in detail.

MAKE EYE CONTACT AND SMILE

Service standard number one is make eye contact and smile. Now this may sound basic and something that every successful business does, right? Have you been to a major fast-food restaurant lately? There is a major fast-food restaurant very near my oldest son's high school. I asked my son Blake if he wanted to stop there with me and get a milkshake. Shockingly, he said yes. I say this because I have recently discovered that my teenage son doesn't think it's cool to hang out with Dad anymore. Now my youngest son still thinks I am cool but not my teenager. As we are leaving the parking lot on our way to enjoy our cool treat, I am humming in my mind the theme song to the 1970s television show *The Courtship of Eddie's Father*, "People, let me tell you about my best friend," when my son snapped me back into reality with his request to only go through the drive-through (he might get seen hanging out with his father). As we approached the drive-through, I was reminded by my son to not mess with the drive-through lady, as I am a teaser by nature. It is important to note before I tell the rest of this story that my children hate to hear about service standards because I constantly lecture them on what went wrong with an experience at a store or restaurant as I am hypersensitive to poor service (a byproduct of speaking about service for the last ten years).

After we ordered our milkshakes, we were greeted (if you could call it a greeting) by a young woman who stuck her arm out the drive-through window with her head looking straight down at the ground and said, "$3.67." There was an awkward four seconds of silence as I waited for her to look at me. My son, knowing that I will not give money to someone until they look at me, was in the passenger seat in a fetal position in an extreme state of embarrassment.

When the young lady finally looked up, I announced in an animated voice, "Eye contact!"

She was so surprised by my comment that she looked at me struggling to think of something to say and finally mumbled, "I'm sorry. I'm about ready to get off work..."

I responded, "That's okay. I will come back fifteen minutes earlier next time so you will look at me." While I was joking with her, I was making a point, and the question here is really very rudimentary—was it her fault that she didn't make eye contact with me? Maybe a little, but remember that young people today do not have the same social skills that older generations had to use to communicate. This is a byproduct of the tools they use to interact with one another. Whether it is Facebook or texting, young people today are not as versed at interpersonal communication skills as older generations. So this must be factored in when hiring them. The real fault in this example lies with the restaurant's management team. The management team did not demand that their drive-through team make eye contact and smile with their guests. While this sounds basic, it is one of the most important elements in human interaction and something you should demand from your team.

GREET AND WELCOME EVERY GUEST

Disney's service standard number 2 is to greet and welcome every guest. My daughter Ashley is a real sweetheart and extremely easy to talk with. She will look you in the eye and smile, ask you about your weekend, and make it very easy to speak with her. My third oldest, Evan, on the other hand is only social if you are a teenage girl. When we bring him to our orthodontist, he looks at the floor the entire way back to the chair. The orthodontic team knows this about Evan, and when he comes in, they crouch down to floor and wave their hands up at him and say hello. He always smiles. What's the point? The Ashleys of the world are easy to connect with, but what is your team doing to connect with the Evans of the world? We must find ways to connect with all customers even the difficult ones. On a sidenote, please make sure your team finds ways to connect with the difficult customers. They tend to be your most loyal. I believe this because most companies or people will not connect with them because they are difficult. I have had many of my clients in the financial service industry tell me how a teller of theirs had really connected with a difficult customer that then would follow that teller when they were transferred to a branch over ten miles away. Those customers would also wait in a line seven people deep even though another teller line became open. Why would they do that? Because that teller had connected with that customer when others couldn't or wouldn't.

SEEK OUT GUEST CONTACT

Disney's principle number 3 is to seek out guest contact. The best way to relate this story to your business is to think of the busiest day you can imagine.

On that day when every member of your team is going one hundred miles per hour remind them to look up and smile at the customers in the lobby or customers on the phone (Yes, you can feel a smile through the phone. Thirty eight percent of our communication has been associated with tone of voice). People will always feel much more special and welcome when we acknowledge them. Mary Kay Ash, founder of Mary Kay Cosmetics, had an experience that makes this point very clearly. Before she was famous, she was standing in a line at a book signing waiting to get a book autographed by one of her favorite writers. When she placed her book in front of the author, the author signed the name of someone else in her book. Ouch! Because of this experience, she had a placard made for her desk that had the initials MMFS (make me feel special). This was a motto she instilled in her associates by ensuring they understood the power of making their customers feel special on an everyday basis.

PROVIDE IMMEDIATE SERVICE RECOVERY

Principle number 4 and one of the most important points in this book has to do with providing immediate service recovery. In fact, it is so important that an entire chapter has been dedicated to this principle. Making mistakes is one of the best times to cement the loyalty of your customer *if*, and the key word here is *if*, you or your team recovers well. We will discuss this in more detail later in the book.

DISPLAY APPROPRIATE BODY LANGUAGE

Principle number 5 in Disney's service standards is to display appropriate body language at all times. Body language is by far the most important element of human communication. In fact, the most widely accepted proof of this comes from a 1967 study by

Albert Mehrabian at UCLA. His research found that an incredible 55 percent of human communication is body language! Another 38 percent is tone. That only leaves 7 percent of communication that is the words we speak. So when someone is interacting with a member of your team, it is the team member's body language and tone that sends 93 percent of the message. While some argue that this is isolated only to communication that is associated with emotion or feelings, it is important to consider this data and remember that your potential client will decide whom she will do business with based on how you and your team make her feel.

Recently, I visited a business in a beautiful suburb of Detroit. As I observed the interaction of the front desk staff member with me and customers, I concluded she must be having a bad day, a bad week, or even a bad year. To say the least, her interpersonal skills were lacking. When I asked the business owner to describe his front desk staff member, he said, "Oh Brenda. She is a real sweetheart once you get to know her." While this sounds funny, it is actually quite dangerous. Wouldn't you rather have someone interacting with your guests and potential customers at the front desk that is a real sweetheart once someone talks to her? If your front desk person is more like the former and less like the latter, that potential client may never get a chance to "get to know her" because they decide to go elsewhere.

PRESERVE THE MAGICAL GUEST EXPERIENCE

Principle number 6 is to preserve the magical guest experience. Here is what the Disney organization knows. They know that when a guest and their family come to Disney, it may be the only vacation they take in a given year. In fact, it may be the only vacation a guest and their family ever take together, so they want to ensure it's magical. There is no reason that in your encounter that the goal should not be the same. No matter if you run a retail business, a dental office, or a government agency, the goal should be to provide an exceptional experience each and every time. To make sure this happens, we must do as former executive vice president of Disney Lee Cockerell says, "I often compare customer service to putting on a show. I tell executives to write a script, hire the best cast to perform it, rehearse it until everyone is razor sharp and then give it your all when the curtain goes up. As a leader, you're the playright, producer, director and you need to have Broadway-level standards to keep your show running to sell-out crowds."

THANK EACH AND EVERY GUEST

The final principle in the Disney service standards relates to gratitude. Thanking each and every guest is a principle we all can relate to as employees, patrons, and parents. To illustrate my point from an employer perspective, I remember having lunch with a very successful orthodontist in the St. Louis area. The doctor was relaying a story about a recent decision he had made to keep his office open on New Year's Eve day. The office staff were not excited about the idea and were pleading with the doctor to close early. He finally gave in and agreed he would close the office at 2:00 p.m. and cater lunch in for his team if they could work through lunch. The doctor catered in a very nice lunch and closed at 2:00 p.m. as he agreed. He felt very disappointed by the whole experience, and being a bit confused, I asked why he felt that way. He said that out of his team of fourteen, only one thanked him for being flexible and also for catering lunch. What's the point? We all know that, as parents, we will do anything for our children, because they are our children. We will, however, do even more if they are appreciative. The book *The Secret* dedicates an entire chapter to the power of gratitude. Please remember this when educating your team on the power a thank-you has on your clients and their willingness to remain your customer and refer their friends.

As a St. Louisan, I would be completely remiss if I did not mention Enterprise Rent-A-Car, one of the greatest companies in the world for customer service. I met Jack Taylor at a very young age and his son and current chairman Andy later in my career. The Taylors focus on providing wow customer service has catapulted the company to the largest rental car company in the world and one of the largest privately held companies in the United States. I cannot tell you the number of times, employees of the company (over seventy thousand employees as of 2010) would tell me how Andy would know their name and even details about their families. Mr. Taylor has always walked the walk when it comes to showing his own employees the power of relationships and making customers and even employees feel special. You should do the same in your business. Your employees always respect what you do more than what you say.

CHAPTER 5

YOUR CUSTOMER'S PERCEPTION IS YOUR COMPANY'S REALITY

COFFEE STAINS

Many people today enjoy the television program *Undercover Boss*. The premise of the show is that the CEO of a prominent corporation goes undercover as an everyday worker to see how his team is treating customers. That same concept was described back in 1982, when Tom Peters wrote a great book called *In Search of Excellence*. The book had many valuable points, but one of the best relates to a president of a European airline that went undercover and sat in coach to see what his patrons experienced. Shortly after takeoff, the attendants had taken drink orders, and the guest next to the airline executive lowered her tray table. To her disgust, she found an ugly coffee stain. After looking at the stain, she looked at the carpet, the luggage compartments, and the rest of the interior of the plane. She then nudged the CEO and said, "If they maintain the engines like they maintain the interior, we are in big trouble." The point of this story is that your client's perception is your company's reality. No matter how good you think your company is at producing a product or service, it will ultimately be judged on the way it is perceived by the customer. What "stains" do you have right now that could be causing your customer to second-guess their decision to do business with you? I recommend that every four to six months, you sit down with your team and ask them to right down every existing stain in your business. They might say things like: stained carpet, clutter, dirty bathroom, delivery times, billing errors, etcetera. Pick these things off one at a time, and those stains will be eliminated from your customer experience. If you do not go through and exercise like this regularly, you run the risk of letting your stains become part of your environment and therefore unseen by your team.

NEVER, NEVER BLAME

In my personal experience, I have noticed that people will more aggressively defend their position when blamed even if they know they are wrong as compared to when they are not blamed. Blaming causes defensiveness whether we are talking about client-staff interactions, staff-staff interactions, or even parent-children encounters. Let me give you an example. There is a very popular television series on the Science Fiction network called *Ghost Hunters*. This show follows a group of former plumbers turned paranormal investigators called TAPS around the country to investigate locations that are supposed to be haunted. This group is coming to my home to investigate our ghost. I called a family meeting to deliver the news that we were going to be famous. When I told my children that TAPS was coming to investigate our home, my youngest child Lance was shocked. He said, "Dad, we have a ghost?" I responded that we not only have a ghost but a poltergeist. "What's that?" he asked me. I told him that it's the type of ghost that does mischievous things like: leaving dirty dishes in the sink, leaving lights on in the basement, and leaving towels on the bathroom floor and cups and plates in the living room.

At this point, my kids all realize that I am being a smart aleck and really talking about all the things that mysteriously happen in our house. You see, my kids spend more time explaining how something was not their fault when blamed than it would take to correct the issue. What's the point? If you blame, be prepared for drama and defensiveness and little, if any, progress. As a sidenote, I had to tell my youngest that we really didn't have a ghost and that we were not going to be on television; he was disappointed.

SELL DON'T TELL

Foundational principle number 2 in communication is to avoid threatening and instead use persuasion to encourage right behaviors. When I was a child, threatening was an everyday tool used by many adults. In fact, in my dentist's office, it was common to scare kids into proper hygiene habits. For example, pointing out the window to the local carnival attraction and asking me if I wanted to become a carnie was a normal way of ensuring that I brushed my teeth. While that approach may have had some effect at producing good oral hygiene, it may also cause psychological damage. (As an adult, I am petrified of toothless people that smell of mushrooms.) We are far better of persuading the behavior we want through education, encouragement, and reward systems.

FOCUS ON WHAT YOU CAN DO, NOT WHAT YOU CAN'T

One of the worst things we can do in a service role is to tell our guest or client what we can't do. It unfortunately happens all the time and turns what could be a positive experience into a negative one simply based on a lack of a good use of common sense and communication skills. To illustrate the point, I recall a recent trip to my daughter's college town.

My daughter Ashley is my wife's best friend, and because of this, she hates it when she leaves each fall for college. In fact, my wife is so close to our daughter she looks for any reason she can to plan a visit to see her. Not too long ago, we had scheduled a trip to see Ashley because it was leaf day. When we visit my daughter, we usually stay the night since it is almost a three-hour trip each way. Although, I travel significantly, the hotel chain I am a premier member with does not have a property in my daughter's college town. So my wife suggested I join the only major chain that has a property in this town of less than twenty thousand.

Within a few months, I not only joined the hotel chain but had reached their highest reward level. Shortly thereafter, we received our first reward night for a free stay. My wife Sharon immediately booked that free night to visit our daughter for the following weekend. The Saturday we chose to visit my daughter was especially ordinary—no football games or parents' day crowds to deal with. The town was abuzz with normality.

Because my wife and daughter are so close (the same relationship my wife has with her own mother), Sharon was eager to get to our daughter's dorm as soon as humanly possible. This eagerness led to our early arrival, some three hours prior to our scheduled 3:00 p.m. check-in time at the hotel. Because we were sleeping over one night, I had packed a small bag with a change of clothes, toiletries, and my favorite pair of man-jams. (Since men don't like to admit they wear pajamas, we make up more masculine names for our nightly garb usually made up of an old college T-shirt and a pair of lounge pants). Sharon, however, had packed two full-size suitcases for this twenty-four-hour stay. Since we were three hours early, my wife was unsure if we would be able to check in early. I on the other hand was completely confident we would be able to check in early especially since we were platinum members, the hotel's highest level of customer tribute.

When we pulled up to the hotel, there were only two cars in the parking lot. Not surprising since this weekend was just an ordinary one with no college celebrations on the calendar. When we entered the lobby, we noticed we were the only people in the front of the hotel, and for that matter, we may have been the only guests in the entire building. After we were acknowledged by the front desk employee, I informed her that we were platinum members and were hoping we could check in early. With that request, we were told and I quote, "Nope, can't do that." You see, we were three hours early and even though there were over seventy-five empty rooms, the front desk employee valued following a hotel rule more than delighting a valued customer. After begging the front desk person to double-check to see if a room was ready, she grumbled off to check, and to our surprise, we were in luck. One of those seventy-five rooms was actually clean and ready even though check-in was not for several hours. The interesting conclusion to this story is this, even though I eventually got what I want (a simple early check-in), I have never been back.

To contrast this experience, let me tell you a great story about my favorite hotel chain Hyatt. As I mentioned earlier, I have four great children: my oldest and very studious Ashley, my strong and kind-hearted son Blake, my football player Evan, and my sweet baby boy Lance. This particular story relates to my son Evan. We had signed him up for Manning Passing Academy in Thibadaux, Louisiana, a twelve-hour drive from our hometown. Fortunately, there was a Hyatt within a very short distance from the football academy. This meant that during our stay, we would be staying in the chain that I used whenever I travel on business. As we mapped out our trip, we decided it would be easier to stay the night in a town a few hours from our final destination the night before camp. As we embarked on our trip, my wife got a call from one of her best friends who informed my wife that the town in which we were spending the night was the murder capital of the South. This caused a major discussion during the rest of the trip as I continued to inform my wife that the town was a very nice town and that the title her friend had given it was unfair and unjustified. As we continued to drive toward our evening's final destination, my wife turned to me and asked me what hotel we were staying in. I explained casually that it was a hotel I had booked off one of those online hotel websites. Knowing that I am frugal, she asked what I had paid for the room. I said they were running a special, and the room cost for the night was $39. She became very nervous and said, "Are you sure this is going to be in a safe neighborhood?"

"Of course," I said. "It will be fine." As we continued to get closer to our hotel room, my wife and I continued to debate how a decent hotel room could be so inexpensive. I continued to assure her that it would be fine. When we finally arrived, we all noticed the bars on all the windows, and I knew this was not going to be pretty. After I rang the bell at the reception area and the hotel employee came out in hair rollers and a bathrobe, I knew I would never hear the end of it. The room was horribly dirty and unkempt, and we of course did not stay. We hurriedly made it back to our car and tiredly began driving the three hours that remained to reach the football camp. Because it was going to be around 3:00 a.m. when we reached Baton Rouge, the location of our Hyatt reservation, I was nervous. We were going to arrive twelve hours before our reservation; I was sure they would not allow us to check in early. When I called to explain what had happened, the Hyatt employee said, "Mr. Johnson, we appreciate your loyalty to our hotel, and we would be glad to check you in early." Now that is outstanding service! So outstanding that I am telling you and everyone I ever speak to about outstanding service. In the grand scheme of things, what did that really cost the hotel? The hotel had the space, and by accommodating me and my family, they made a lifetime customer of me. Well worth the cost of bending a few rules to wow the guest.

PHRASES TO AVOID

As discussed previously, body language and tone of voice are very powerful tools used in human communications and, in most cases, have more impact than words. However, adding the wrong words with a negative tone or body language is an absolute recipe for disaster. Below are listed phrases that tend to make customers defensive.

Phrase Number 1: Are You Sure?

Has anyone ever uttered the words, "Are you sure?" to you? How did it make you feel? Most likely those words made you feel not believed and, in some cases, caused you to second-guess yourself. The phrase can never be taken any way but negatively, so ensure your team avoids it at all costs.

Phrase Number 2: What's the Problem This Time?

"What the problem this time?" If you are a teaser and your customer knows that you are a teaser, this phrase or similar joking with the client can actually be an icebreaker. If however, your customer does not know this about you or your staff member, they will never talk to you again, so be careful with sarcasm. Your better to avoid it than run the risk of being misunderstood.

Phrase Number 3: No One Else Has Complained

In many businesses today, leaders have spent hundreds or even thousands of hours ensuring that their company provides an excellent product or service. This of course is absolutely critical and should always be at the center of what we do as leaders. That being said, I have seen many companies make the mistake of pointing this out to their customer during a service mistake. The problem is that the pointing this out to a disappointed customer serves no value. They honestly do not care that you have provided a service or product 3,911 times in a row correctly. They are only concerned at that moment with *their* experience. Please remember that pointing out that no one else has complained comes across defensive and uncaring.

Phrase Number 4: Who Told You That?

A pattern is obviously developing here. Defensiveness never leads to connectivity with your customer. This statement is one of the worst because it not only implies the customer is not believed but also that the person who may have informed them is not credible.

Phrase Number 5: It's Not My Job

While it is exceptionally rare for one of your staff members to utter these words to a customer, their body language might be exuding these feelings. So they need to be very careful what message they are letting their nonverbal language send. It is however more common for your staff members to develop an attitude of "It is not my job" while interacting with other teammates. They spend a lot of time together and can become somewhat intolerant of each other if you don't make time to work on team building as an office. It is very important that you teach your employees to gently confront each other when dealing with conflict. This concept comes from clinical psychologist Dr. Terry Paulson. In his workshop called the "Assertiveness Advantage," he describes how teaching your team to *gently confront* will teach them to talk to one another and not about one another. Terry may be the world's best trainer I have ever seen in teaching your team to *gently confront.*

Phrase Number 6: It's Company Policy

The absolute worst thing your staff member can say to a customer is the phrase, "It's company policy." These words elicit angry feelings from your client and make them feel like they are being "processed," not served. Let me explain how following company policies can alienate the very people you are trying to service. My wife is beloved by everyone. She is sweet, kindhearted, thoughtful, loyal, and, most especially, nonconfrontational. She is so nonconfrontational that she will usually make me handle any situation that could turn into a conflict. The only exception to this rule is if she feels her children need to be defended, at which point she turns from Mary Poppins to Sarah Connor from the movie the *Terminator*. A couple of years ago, my son Evan was begging my wife to take him to the local recreation center that we were members of to play basketball. She had a very busy morning planned and informed

Evan that the only way she could bring him was if she dropped him off while she ran her errands, and he could only spend about an hour and a half there. My son was more than willing to accept these terms and asked if he could bring a friend with him. My wife agreed, and off they went to the recreation center.

As my wife went to check in the boys, my son's friend Christian looked up at my wife and said he was not a member. My wife, who hates to disappoint, was now in panic mode. She had no cash on her and knew that the recreation center did not take credit cards. As she frantically dug through her purse, hoping to find a 5-dollar bill, she remembered that she had an unused gift card for thirty dollars from a birthday party that was planned at the center but not held. She asked the person at the counter if the gift card could be used to pay the five dollars admission fee for my son's friend. The center employee informed her that using the gift card would be an acceptable form of payment.

Now, feeling relieved, my wife handed the employee the gift card and gave the boys their final instructions before leaving to run her errands. "Excuse me," said the recreation center staff member. "This card is expired. Our company policy clearly states that we do not accept expired gift cards." Normally, as I mentioned earlier, my wife will avoid conflict, but this involved one of her children, so she was willing to confront. She asked for the manager expecting that the person in charge would surely see that this policy was silly. When the manager came out, she told my wife that the employee was correct and that the policy was the policy. At this point, my wife became very annoyed. She cleared her throat and did her best Perry Mason impersonation. For those of you reading this book too young to know who Perry Mason was, he was a character on a 1960s television series about a trial lawyer. If you know anything about trial lawyers, you know they will never put you on the witness stand and ask you any question that they don't already know the answer.

My wife went on to ask her series of questions to the manager of the center. Questions like, "How long have we been members here?" Knowing the answer was three years. "How do we pay?" Knowing that we had the fifty-four dollars per month fee automatically deducted from our checking account. "How often do we use the facility?" Knowing that we used the facility very sparingly. After these series of questions, my wife asked the manager if it was a good policy to invalidate a thirty-dollar gift card that we paid cash for only a couple of months ago when considering we were members in good standing for over three years that paid excellent and barely used the facility. After considering my wife's well laid out argument, the recreation center manager agreed to make an exception to the policy but said that she was going to "note" in our account that she was doing us a favor. This of course infuriated my wife.

At the end of the day, I had travelled home from a long business trip. I had debated that night if I should just spend that night or drive the five plus hours home and arrive around midnight. I decided to drive home that night. When I opened the garage door at some time near midnight, my wife was standing at the door to greet me. She could not wait to tell me how embarrassed and upset she was at the way she was treated at the recreation center. After listening to her story, she asked me to cancel the membership. The next morning, I called and cancelled the membership, and no one and I mean no one tried to stop me. The employee at the center was more than glad to "process" my request. They simply did not care.

Unfortunately for them, I have told that story to over one thousand people in seminars within a ten-mile radius of that facility, and I mentioned the facility name each time I told my story. As business leaders, we need to be sure our employees know it is okay to bend the rules when it is in the best interest of the business or just as importantly, the customer.

CHAPTER 6

USE MISTAKES TO CEMENT LOYALTY

It is a wonderful goal to try and provide an outstanding experience for the customer each and every time they do business with you and your company. This fantastic experience, while important, is not nearly as powerful as the impact of fixing a mistake. The reason is simply because most of us as consumers are accustomed to being underwhelmed when something goes wrong with a service experience. We deal with an apathetic employee who does not care whether we are upset, disappointed, or willing to take our business elsewhere. We try and escalate the issue to an employee that is a supervisor or manager only to find a similar lack of empathy toward our circumstance.

Research shows that very few companies have trained their employees on how to fix mistakes. This means that when something goes wrong with a customer, employees in most organizations tend to wing it instead of following a technique or system that has been proven to wow the guest.

Frederick Reicheld in his book *The Loyalty Effect* describes the impact that recovering from mistakes can have on your customer's loyalty. He indicates that recovering well and doing so immediately can have a bigger impact then providing the perfect experience.

The reason for this is that the customer is expecting their service or product to go off without a hitch. What the consumer is not prepared for is to be overwhelmed with how a mistake is fixed. In fact, most consumers are used to being disappointed when a mistake occurs with a service experience.

In order to provide a great opportunity to recover from a mistake, your team must have a system they follow to ensure they are consistent. A proven system also ensures that the steps they follow will work almost every time. Below is an outline of a simple four-step system that has been implemented by many of the best companies around the world.

1. Apologize empathetically
2. Fix the problem not the blame
3. Do something extra
4. Have a leader follow up

APOLOGIZE EMPATHETICALLY

Step number 1 is very critical and sets up the other three. Apologizing with empathy carries a great deal of power. Empathy allows your staff member to *feel with* your guest and is very different than apologizing with sympathy. Sympathy or feeling *for* someone has about a tenth of the strength of empathy. When we are able to feel *with* our guest, we are literally jumping into their shoes with them. Saying something like, "I am so sorry we did not have you in the appointment calendar. I know how hard it is for you to get off work," is strongly empathetic and allows your customer to feel as though you understand their circumstance. Train your team to handle these situations by role playing with them. Listen for the empathy and discuss as a team what was done well and what might need improvement. I cannot overemphasize the importance of role playing. Initially, your team will resist it, but I know of no better way to ensure the skills you require are being done and sound polished.

FIX THE PROBLEM NOT THE BLAME

In almost every case, your customer simply wants their problem solved and solved quickly. The second step allows them to see that the staff member at your company is taking ownership of the issue and not passing the buck. It is very frustrating for us as consumers to be explaining our problem to a person that is not willing as a member of the organization that wronged us to be empathetic to our issue and not willing to take ownership of the mistake. The customers of your business are the responsibility of everyone from the front desk person all the way to the business owner. If someone in accounting messed up, we should own that mistake just the same as if we had made the mistake ourselves. The customer does not care who is at fault; they just want their problem fixed and fixed fast.

DO SOMETHING EXTRA

After your staff has apologized to the customer and fixed their problem, step 3 is to do something extra. This is truly where magic can happen and, if done correctly, can turn a negative experience into a wow experience. The best organization on the planet at doing something extra is Disney. They are so good at it that several real examples of Disney examples will follow. Remember that fixing mistakes is an opportunity to cement loyalty at a level greater than if everything went perfectly with the experience.

Several years ago, I was conducting a seminar on this topic in St. Louis, Missouri, to a group of about 120 dentists and dental staff. At the end of the event, one of the office managers from a large dental group came up to share her Disney experience with me.

During the prior year, she, her husband, and two children planned a trip to Disney in Orlando. They had never been to the Magic Kingdom, and they were all very eager to enjoy the experience. While they were planning to visit the parks over several days, they decided not to have their overnight accommodations at one of the Disney resorts. Instead, they planned to stay at a major hotel chain that the husband was a platinum member of so that they could take advantage of the free suite they received whenever they went on vacation. They always got free accommodations because he stays with the hotel chain over 150 nights per year.

The hotel was about ten minutes from the park, and they had purchased special tickets to Disney that allowed them to enter the theme park thirty minutes before the general public so that several rides could be enjoyed without lines. The kids, she explained, were ecstatic about this option of early arrival and had mapped out what rides they could go on the night before their first day visit to the park. The following morning, she recalled was like a movie scene. The temperature in Orlando was going to be in the midseventies and not a cloud was forecasted. All the flowers in Orlando were in bloom, and the day truly felt as though it was going to be magical. The office manager went on to tell me that she decided to wear her brand-new white Capri pants to the park that day. As they arrived at the gates of Disney on the hotel shuttle, the office manager felt her entire bottom was wet. When she got up to leave, she looked at her behind and found that someone had poured an entire cup of black coffee in her seat. As you can imagine, the stain on the backside of her white Capri pants was awful, and she was terribly embarrassed. At this point, most people would hurriedly get back on the shuttle and return to the hotel for a new pair of pants. But being the martyr that most moms are when it comes to their children, she decided to "grin and bear it" so that her kids would not miss out on their early entry tickets.

When they arrived at the front gates, the ticket taker noticed the office manager's pants and did what all Disney cast members are trained to do: provide immediate service recovery. The Disney employee asked what had happened. After learning of the coffee incident, she came out from the ticket counter and escorted the family to the closest Disney apparel store. She then explained what had happened and told the apparel employee to allow the guest to pick out any pair of shorts or pants she would like and Disney would pick up the cost. That is incredible, but it gets better. The ticket taker then tells the office manager and her family they would now be VIP guests and would get to go in the front of every line and lead Mickey in the parade on Main Street later that afternoon. Now that is a wow experience of epic proportions!

After telling this story to thousands of attendees at my workshops, I had a person come up to me after a seminar and say, "I have that story beat!" Always interested in adding great stories to my seminars, I asked her to share. She said that several years prior, they had taken their then seven-year-old daughter Sophia to Disney. Sophia was extremely excited and could not wait to see some of her favorite characters especially Tigger from Winnie the Pooh. Literally, minutes after arriving at the park, Sophia had spied a stuffed Tigger in the store near the entrance of the park. This was a special Tigger to her because it was pink, and she had never seen a pink Tigger before. She begged and begged her parents to buy that special pink Tigger. Because it was the first day of the trip, they hesitated but finally gave in. She named the pink Tigger Tanya. She took it on every ride that day and absolutely loved her new friend. That evening, after a long day of rides, they decided to have dinner in the back section of the park. After a wonderful dinner and near closing time, the family left the restaurant and made their way back to the shuttle. Suddenly, Sophia cried out, "Tanya! I forgot Tanya!" If you are a parent, I am sure you would have done what this couple did. They jumped off the shuttle and ran back to the restaurant hoping they would get there before it closed. Unfortunately, they did not. Sophia was devastated. The parents called the Wilderness Lodge, a Disney property, they were staying at and explained what had happened and asked if there were any way to get back into the restaurant. The Disney resort employee empathized with the guest (step number 1) and then said she had a solution to the problem (step number 2). She then encouraged the parents to come back to the resort. Less than thirty minutes later, when the couple arrived back at their hotel room, there on the bed was an exact twin to Tanya Tigger along with a note made out to Sophia. The note said she had gotten lost, but Disney found her and brought her back (step number 3). This was an incredibly powerful recovery by Disney and one of the best stories I have ever heard on fixing a mistake or problem a guest experienced; simply incredible.

HAVE A LEADER FOLLOW-UP

One of the most powerful ways to cement the loyalty of a customer is to have a key leader personally follow-up. The follow-up should occur after the first three steps are completed and should definitely be done by someone in the organization that has a position of authority (preferably the business owner). The follow-up can be done by phone, e-mail, or even by snail mail, but the key is that a person in leadership initiates the interaction. If someone else does the follow-up, it still has power, but ultimately, your client will think that person is simply following a procedure. If a key leader or the business owner follows up, the customer believes he or she truly cares. Please be sure your team feels comfortable telling you a mistake occurred so that you can take advantage of this wonderful bonding opportunity.

CHAPTER 7

ASK THE ONE QUESTION THAT CAN TRANSFORM YOUR BUSINESS

Today, your customers are inundated with information—junk mail, e-mail, texts, phone solicitors, the list goes on and on. The last thing we should do is become more white noise by sending out surveys that are too long and, in some cases, irrelevant to the experience. Frederick Reicheld, one of the world's absolute experts on customer loyalty, conducted research to determine what question or questions were best to ask when surveying customers. In his book *The Ultimate Question*, he discusses his findings that have incredible implications to your business should you decide to act on them. Reicheld found that there is actually one question, when held in isolation, tells you the business owner or business leader, everything you need to know about the state of your company.

The only question you need to be asking according to Reicheld's research is this: *How likely is it that you would refer us to a friend or colleague?* Reicheld used a scale of 0 to 10 for possible client responses as illustrated below:

How likely is it that you would refer us to a friend or colleague?

10 9 8 7 6 5 4 3 2 1 0

Extremely Likely — Not Likely

His research finds that customers that score your company from 0-6 are actively disparaging your business. They tell friends verbally that they don't like your company and may tell the whole world this by writing negative reviews on sites like Google Review, Yelp, and others. This group is referred to by Reicheld as detractors. In general, you may have a very small percentage of clients that fall into this category, but you should not let that lull you to sleep. It only takes a few very upset customers to cause a major ripple effect in how business is perceived especially if they are technology savvy.

The second group that Reicheld identifies is called promoters. This group score a 9 or higher on the continuum and are absolute cheerleaders of your company. They will tell everyone how great you are and are significant contributors to the growth of your business as it relates to referrals.

The third group identified score a business a 7 or 8 on the question of likelihood of referring a friend or colleague. This group is actually neutral in their feelings, and while they like your business just fine, they are not likely to refer you often. This group in most cases will represent a huge opportunity for growth if you can turn them into promoters. In fact, Reicheld's research found that by increasing your promoters by 12 percent, your growth will double! That is incredible return on investment for wowing your clients. The catch is that moving these neutral customers to delighted ones is a lot of work. It means that members of your team need to provide a Disney-like experience every day and every encounter.

Is it worth it? The research says yes. Remember that as the leader of your company, you set the tone and the tempo. I have visited with many business owners doing the things discussed in this book, and they are achieving incredible results and growth.

PART TWO

CREATING AN ARMY OF OWNERS

I have spent a great portion of this book describing what things constitute a wow experience. Not that we have established the *what* that needs to be done to create a magical customer encounter; we must put in place the necessary systems to ensure that your team implements these ideas on a regular basis, over and over and again and again. Without consistency and repetition, everything in this book is purely theoretic. To ensure that we make the things discussed in this book a reality, the leadership team of your company has five things they must ensure occur. These five things are laid out in each of the last five chapters.

CHAPTER 8

SETTING CLEAR EXPECTATIONS

Set clear expectations; sounds easy, doesn't it? I mean who doesn't set clear expectations? Well, according to the book *First Break All the Rules*, over half of our employees would not strongly agree with the statement, "I clearly understand what is expected of me at work." That to me is a mind-blowing statistic. I sure hope that if I ever have to go into surgery, I get the 50 percent of the medical staff that can strongly agree with this statement.

Whenever I conduct workshops on this subject, I always ask the attendees to write down the answers to the following questions:

1. What is your job?
2. What are the top three priorities of your job?

For question number 1, almost the entire audience will give me a job title. This of course really only tells me their area of responsibility. It really doesn't tell me their job. When I tell them that they seem to get my point. Your job in a business focused on an incredible customer experience is to wow. That "wow" must happen on three very important levels. To be successful long term in any organization, it is imperative to wow the leadership team, and most people get that. Another area that an employee must wow is the customer, and again most people get that.

But just as important as these two elements is the necessity to wow teammates. Without this third element, we have a two-legged barstool, and two-legged barstools don't stand. I have been in many companies consulting over the last ten years that have a key employee or two that are two-legged barstools. Leadership and customers love them, but they are terrible teammates. Here is my opinion on these people—they have to go. Even if they are productive members of your team, the amount of poison they spread throughout your organization is not worth it. As Jim Collins said in his book *Good to Great*, "Get the right people on the bus and the wrong people off."

When I ask for the answer to the next question, I get all kinds of answers. Most of which are task-related. Don't get me wrong; we all have important tasks that must get done in our jobs, but I am looking for deeper answers here. When I have interviewed top leaders across various industries and ask them what they think the top priorities of great employees should be, I get three answers that come up more frequently than any others. The number 1 answer by far is a great attitude. I completely agree with those that say you must hire for talent first, but talent with a poor attitude will never work out long term. Intuitively, this makes sense, but various research done at the university level has actually backed it up. Attitude and optimism have been linked to significantly higher productivity (by up to 31 percent) as discussed by Harvard researcher Shawn Achor in his book *The Happiness Advantage.*

The second of the three critical priorities of a great employee is being a great team player. Research at the university level has also substantiated the impact of strong team environments. In fact, a study done in 2008 by Kathryn Shaw of Stanford found teams can increase productivity especially when dealing with complex problems when they shared meaningful incentives, knew management would listen to them, and had an environment that encouraged teamwork.

In my opinion, you must first have the right team players on the team, or no matter how great the environment is for teamwork, the team won't function properly. That is why a great attitude must be the first priority followed by an environment that is designed for teamwork.

The third of the three priorities of great employees is having the ability to wow. This was mentioned earlier but cannot be emphasized enough. First as employers, we must hire people that are talented with great attitudes and who are also great teammates, but they also must have the ability and willingness to wow the customer. Usually, the first two priorities of great attitude and willingness to be a team player take care of the third. However, they are all truly critical and symbiotic if you want long-term employees that make a huge impact with your customers every day.

Now that we have established the three priorities of an employee: have a great attitude even when you don't feel like it, be a great team player because the company will provide a great team environment, and, lastly, go out of your way as an employee to wow the customer each and every day, we as leaders must ensure our employees know these are the things we covet through our actions and communications each and every day. One of the ways to do this is sit down with your employees collectively and one on one and explain that these three things they will be measured on, rewarded on, and promoted on now and into the future. You then must make sure that your feedback including performance reviews, scoreboards, and one-on-one meetings reflect this philosophy.

Now that we have covered the big picture items, we cannot ignore the day-to-day things we expect from our team. One of the best ways to ensure daily expectations are met is to hold huddle meetings. This is a short five to ten minutes each morning to remind everyone what is important for that day's success. The meeting's name is derived from the game of football. A morning huddle is intended to be short and to the point; in fact, some companies I have met with conduct the meeting standing up just like a real huddle.

Another important element of setting clear expectations may sound counterintuitive. Be sure to set clear expectations on the *results you expect*, but give them latitude in *how* they achieve those results. What I mean by this is micromanaging every step they take can work, but it limits your team's ability to think for themselves and use creativity to solve customer problems. Be sure your team knows what is acceptable and what their boundaries are and then get out of the way and let them own the customer experience at their level. I mentioned a story earlier about a woman who stained her pants on her way to Disney. The Disney employee who wowed her did not go ask a supervisor if it was okay to leave her post. The Disney employee did not get permission to offer to buy her a new pair of shorts and make them a VIP family. She just did it. This is a classic example of setting the expectation of the end result and giving your employees the latitude to make it happen.

Ultimately, at the end of the day, you as the business leader create the culture, set the expectations, and, therefore, dictate the customer experience. If you are not providing and incredible experience for your customer with each and every encounter, it is not your employee's fault. They do not have the power to dictate culture. Surely they can influence it, but you as the leader absolutely shape the environment. Just remember what Captain Abrashoff did on the *USS Benfold* in a very short time. It begins and ends at the top. Be the type of leader that walks the walk not just talks the talk.

CHAPTER 9

PEOPLE ONLY RESPECT WHAT YOU INSPECT

It is always interesting to ask attendees in my workshops the question, "Have you ever worked with someone who was not doing the things they needed to for your business to be successful?" I always get interesting answers to this question, things like laziness, bad attitude, and stubbornness come up very frequently. The most common answer

I receive is lack of accountability. Interesting because this would be the same reason I would give if I was asked that question. The main reason your employees are violating the things that you covet is because *you* let them.

Let me use a popular television show about animals to make my point about acceptable and unacceptable behavior. Caesar Milan is a dog behaviorist and has a show on the National Geographic network called *The Dog Whisperer*. On the show, Caesar is called to various homes of people that have out of control dogs. Almost invariably, the show's producers choose people that have very successful business or professional lives: lawyers, doctors, business owners, and even one show that focused on a psychiatric nurse with dog problems.

The dogs picked for the show are usually very out of control. When Caesar arrives, he is told by the owner what the problem is with their family canine. No matter what the problem, Caesar listens intently and then informs the dog owners that they don't have a dog problem. The dog owners always look confused when he says that and strongly argue how crazy their dog has become. Caesar waits for them to finish and then says, "You don't have a dog problem. You have a people problem. The reason your dog chases the mailman is because you let him." Caesar explains that dogs are pack animals, and they will do or won't do what the alpha dog allows. If the family dog thinks it is the alpha dog because of the behaviors it has gotten a way with, the more time it will take to teach the pet that the people are in charge. By the end of the show, Caesar has retrained the dog and has educated the dog owners on the proper pack behavior. Now what can we as business leaders learn from a dog trainer about managing people? We can learn that humans will behave in ways that their human pack leader says is okay. So if coming in late is tolerated, then people will come in late. If being a poor team player has no consequence, then some members of your team will not work at being team players, and the consequence is bad team dynamics. You are your team's ultimate alpha, and you must set clear expectations and hold your team accountable to those standards. People will most respect those things that we as leaders follow up on and reward or recognize.

CHAPTER 10

PUT PEOPLE IN ROLES THAT ACCENTUATE THEIR STRENGTHS

A great deal of research has been done over the last few years focused on the power of putting people in roles that allow them to utilize their strengths. Historically, however, business leaders have spent countless hours trying to help employees improve their weaknesses. Business leaders have also spent a great deal of time trying to fix employees that were not meeting their expectations. Thousands of dollars were spent and hours and hours of time were labored with usually poor results. Why? Because many times we have the wrong people in the wrong roles, and in some cases, we just simply have the wrong people. This does not mean that they are bad people, just bad fits.

In the NFL, this would never happen the way it happens in business. Teams spend hundreds if not thousands of hours scouting their top draft pick in the yearly draft. They interview them, test them, time them, compare them, and watch video on them to be sure that their potential draft pick is a good risk. If they were doing all this research and investment to draft a quarterback for example, they would not then move that quarterback to defensive tackle. It just would not make sense to move a 225-pound quarterback that spent ten thousand hours of his life training to throw footballs to a position in which the average player is 60 pounds heavier and spent the same ten thousand hours learning to tackle and block people. Yet business leaders have been filling positions with wrong people for years and getting frustrated when those people don't perform well.

As business leaders, we must make sure we have our best players on the field every day. No position should ever be taken for granted. Our front-line people need to be just as skilled as our top position in the company. Unfortunately, many companies just fill front-line positions with a warm body and then wonder why their service suffers or their business lacks growth.

So now that we have established the critical nature of identifying strengths of your team members, how do you actually go about doing it? There are many tools both intuitive and scientific that can be used. I will break these down over the next few pages.

ASK THEM

The first thing I suggest is simply ask your team members what they feel are their strengths. While this is the least reliable methodology, it does give you a foundation from which to start. The reason I say it is the least reliable is because surprisingly most people are not very self-aware. Even though this methodology is not as accurate as those mentioned later in this section, it still is very valuable exercise for several reasons. It shows that you care about them, and this by itself has great benefits. Another reason this exercise is good to conduct is because they may discover that you think they are good at things they did not mention. Lastly, conducting this exercise lets your team know that you value understanding what each member does well. This helps you to use that feeling of value as you position your organization to be "strength-organized" in the future with far less resistance.

OBSERVATION AND ASKING OTHERS

Another valuable exercise in determining employee strengths is to simply watch them or ask their teammates what they think they are really good at doing. Again, while this is not scientific, it does provide valuable insight as to what duties or assignments employees flourish at performing.

STRENGTH ASSESSMENTS

There has been a lot of research conducted recently on the value of determining strengths and using formalized assessments to do so. Two of the best and most reliable systems I have seen are DISC and Strength Finders 2.0. DISC has been in use for over thirty years and is a behavior assessment tool based on the work of psychologist Dr. William Marston. The system is based on four primary personality types: dominant, influence, steadiness, and conscientiousness. After completing an online assessment that asks the participant to answer a twenty-eight-question test, a detailed twenty plus page report is created explaining in detail how the employee is effectively hardwired. It is really great, and I highly recommend it. The assessments are also very economical. The DISC Classic can be done for less than $30 an employee.

Strength Finder 2.0, a book written by Tom Rath, is another great tool that also provides and online assessment that identifies and employee's top five strengths. This tools was developed based on research done by the Gallup organization and is also a phenomenal tool that can be done for less than $30 an employee.

According to the research done by Gallup, the return on investment derived from structuring your organization for strengths is incredible. In his book *Now, Discover Your Strengths*, Marcus Buckingham states that the research showed that employees that could strongly agree that they have the opportunity to do what they are best every day at work were up to 38 percent more productive and up to 44 percent more likely to work in business units with higher customer satisfaction scores. If that does not convince you that you should be putting your employees in roles that accentuate their strengths, nothing will.

CHAPTER 11

CONNECT WITH EMPLOYEES AND CUSTOMERS

One of my favorite seminars to conduct is on connection. When I say connection, I mean finding a way to truly bond with your employee or customer. I am not talking about being a good public speaker or writing well;

although those skills are tremendous assets. What I am describing with the word connection is the unique ability that some people have to make you feel like they really know you even though you have only just met them.

Dr. Mark Goulston, MD, is an expert on communication and one of the world's most sought after authorities on listening. In fact, when the FBI trains hostage negotiators, Dr. Goulston is their man. He has a best-selling book on the topic of listening called *Just Listen* that is a phenomenal resource to improve your skills as a great connector. I say this because in order to be a great connector, you must first be a great listener. According to Dr. Goulston, not only are most people bad listeners, but we are also very quick to make judgments about the people we do meet and let those perceptions cloud our ability to really hear what the person is saying. In other words, we judge the people we are interacting with and allow that judgment to influence our willingness to listen. I have said to my audiences in workshops, "Would I be as believable talking about business improvement strategies if I came out to speak in a tank top and cutoffs and had a nose ring versus a business suit?" Now, this may sound like a silly example, but we allow our perceptions to influence our willingness to listen all the time. Be careful not to let your perception cloud your own willingness to listen.

To be a great connector, we must first learn to become great listeners, and listening truly is a skill. Remember that great listeners, *listen to understand not to respond*. This sounds basic, but if you are not careful, you will do the opposite. Here is why. The average person can speak at a rate of 120–150 words per minute. The average person can think at a rate of 500–1,000 words per minute. This leaves the brain with a whole lot of time to be thinking about something else during a conversation, things like, "Who is picking the kids up?" or "I have to make sure I get that e-mail sent before I go home." These distractions can cause you to seem uninterested or preoccupied, and you might miss your opportunity to truly understand the person speaking with you, or they simply shut down. One of the best resources on the planet to improve your listening skills is Dr. Goulston's book. I highly recommend you use it to improve your and your team's listening skills. Don't take this incredibly powerful skill for granted; it is the most important skill in connecting with others.

So other than great listening, what do great connectors do to connect? Nido Qubein, one of the world's foremost authorities on communication, says they ask more questions than they make statements. As leaders, I think we have a tendency to do the opposite. I believe that most of the best ideas to improve your company are in the minds of your employees doing the work every day. All you have to do is ask them. If you do this, be prepared for the truth. I say this because every leader is not willing to hear the truth and can cause more harm than good. Let me give you an example of how this can backfire.

Several years ago, I was conducting a small workshop in a client's office. One of the exercises I conducted required the office staff to describe coffee stains that could cause the customers to form a bad impression of the company. Eager to perform this exercise, the team discussed what they felt were issues that could cause a negative impression of the business. As they did this, the business owner sat with me and waited for their answer. At the end of the exercise, the team had identified the high temperature in the building to be a coffee stain. "That's ridiculous," said the business owner. "Our temperature is just fine." The team of employees looked as though they had just been scolded, and from that point on, they were unwilling to say what was truly on their mind. As a sidenote, I was conducting the seminar in their office and sweating profusely.

Remember, if you are going to ask for the truth, be prepared to hear it.

Great connectors also make the person they are interacting with truly feel special. This trait is the same in every great connector I have ever met. It is the ability to make the other person feel like they are the only person in the room. This means they ignore text messages or phone calls when interacting with someone. They lean forward and display body language that says they are waiting on the edge of their seat to hear the next thing that person says in the conversation. They truly act interested in learning that person's point of view. The best story to make this point comes from the business classic book *How to Win Friends and Influence People* written by Dale Carnegie. He speaks of being at a cocktail party in which he was cornered by a gentleman who began speaking about his own career of which Carnegie was no expert. So Carnegie simply employed the skills mentioned above. He listened intently. Several weeks later, Carnegie received a letter in the mail from the gentleman from the party telling Carnegie what a great conversationalist he was. Carnegie said that during the entire conversation, he might have said only a few sentences! The rest of the time, he was listening intently, acting truly engaged, and making the person feel special.

The last point I want to make about connecting has to do with truly being happy for others and the success they are having in their life. Too often, humans compare themselves to others and, in some cases, become spiteful if someone they know is having success in some part of their life. My all-time favorite story that demonstrates this point comes from arguably the greatest motivational speaker of all time, Zig Ziglar. Zig told a story in one of his workshops about his love for golf. He loved the game, but because of the time it took, he felt guilty missing the time with this family. One day, he had an epiphany—the best way to play golf and spend time with this family would be to turn his wife and eleven-year-old son Tom into golfing buddies. So Zig bought each a new set of clubs, and off they went to play golf together. Several rounds into this new family adventure, his wife approached Zig and said while she loved spending time with him and Tom, golf just was not for her. So Zig lost golfing buddy number 1.

Not too long after that, Zig's son, Tom, approached him and delivered the same news as his mother. There went golfing buddy number 2. Several years later, Tom and Zig were out to dinner and Tom asked Zig if he wanted to stop at the driving range and hit some golf balls. Zig jumped at the chance, and off they went. At the range, Tom used one of his father's clubs and hit one of the best shots ever. He was so excited they decided to go to the golf course several days later and play a round of golf. On one of the golf holes, Zig's son again borrowed his father's golf club and hit the perfect shot. He followed up that shot with another beautiful shot that landed forty feet from the hole. After Zig helped line him up, Tom hit his putt and sank the putt for a birdie, one shot better than par. Both Tom and Zig jumped straight in the air and did a victory dance. Then Zig thought about his next shot and remembered he was also putting for birdie. He debated whether he should purposely miss the putt but then thought this would not be right because he would give his son a cheap victory. So Zig lined up his putt and gave it his best effort, and as luck would have it, the ball went straight in the hole for a birdie. Zig looked at Tom and said, "Son, tell me the truth. Were you pulling for Dad?"

Tom looked at his father and said, "Dad, I am always pulling for you." I almost cry every time I hear that story. That, ladies and gentlemen, is true happiness for the success of others. If we could have more of this feeling in our communities, families, and business, we would definitely be the better for it.

Great connectors listen well, ask more questions than they make statements, make people feel special, and, lastly, they truly are happy for others and their success.

CHAPTER 12

RECOGNIZE AND REWARD RIGHT BEHAVIORS

This is such an appropriate section to conclude this book because it truly is the ingredient that makes the whole recipe of building a wow organization come together. Whenever I lecture on this topic, I ask my audience to tell me by a show of hands how important recognition is to employees. When I ask the audience if it is an 8 or higher, every hand in the room goes up. When I ask if it is a 9 or higher, every hand stays up. In fact, I almost always have someone yell out, "It is an 11!" Interestingly, there is finally scientific research that backs up the power of recognition and feedback. The book *The Twelve Elements of Great Managing* references a study done in 1998 in London that asked participants to play a video game in which they were rewarded for each level of advancement through the game that they had achieved. The participants were then hooked up to sensors so their brain activity could be measured. The brain activity when achievement was reached showed dopamine levels increased to a level similar to that observed following an intravenous injection of amphetamine. This is scientific evidence for what great leaders have known intuitively for years: recognition works, and it does so on a physiological level.

An anecdotal story is a great way to close this section and actually to end this book. I can think of no better story I have heard that demonstrates the power of praise than the one that follows. Several years ago, a very famous movie star was being interviewed in *Parade* magazine. This movie star was one of my favorites from my childhood. In his prime, this star was very unique because his popularity was generationally universal. Old people loved him because he was charming. Women loved him because he was good-looking. Men loved him because he was a man's man and in real life one of the toughest men in Hollywood. Children loved him because he was funny and as cool as the other side of the pillow. This star was at one point one of the most recognizable names in the world.

Toward the twilight of his career, *Parade* magazine interviewed him. The reporter interviewing him was also a huge fan and asked him all kinds of great questions. What was his favorite movie? What was his greatest moment? How did he break into Hollywood? The interview was going great and very lighthearted until the reporter asked him what was his greatest regret in life. This macho, tough man's man could not immediately answer the question. The reason he could not was because he was fighting back the tears that were filling his eyes. As he gained his composure, he answered the reporter's question. He said that he grew up in the South. He said that in the town he grew up in his father was the chief of police and one of the most respected men in the whole county. He said that in the South, a boy does not become a man until his father tells him he is a man. He went on to say that his father never told him he was a man and never told him he was proud of him. That was this world famous actor's greatest regret. Not the part in a movie he didn't get or the bad investment he made. His greatest regret was that his father wasn't proud of him. I fight back the tears every time I hear this story.

As I mentioned earlier in the book, many of you reading this have father wounds, and I am truly sorry for that but can personally not change that. Many of your employees have father wounds, and you personally can't change that. What you can do however is make sure they don't develop boss wounds. Remind them often how much you care about them and appreciate them, for nothing in this book can become a reality without great people on your team. Great people that work in an environment that creates a wow experience both for the customer and the team members will make you proud each and every day. You are only as good as those who work for you. Hire great talent, create a great atmosphere, set the expectations clearly, and watch the magic happen. Good luck with your business, and remember what Zig Ziglar said to close many of his workshops and was the title of one his best-selling books, "See you at the top!"